# ANCIENT
# China

by Natalie M. Rosinsky

**Content Adviser:**
Hanchao Lu, PhD, Professor
School of History, Technology & Society
Georgia Institute of Technology

COMPASS POINT BOOKS
a capstone imprint

Compass Point Books
1710 Roe Crest Drive
North Mankato, MN 56003
www.capstonepub.com

Managing Editor: Catherine Neitge
Designers: Heidi Thompson and Lori Bye
Media Researcher: Eric Gohl
Library Consultant: Kathleen Baxter
Production Specialist: Laura Manthe

**Image Credits**
Art Resource, N.Y.: Erich Lessing, 30, SEF, 32; Bridgeman Art Library: Archives Charmet, 29,
Giraudon, 26, Victoria & Albert Museum, London, U.K., 34; Getty Images: SSPL, 17, Time & Life
Pictures/Howard Sochurek, 21, Universal History Archive, 42; iStockphotos: hudiemm, 22, Torsten
Stahlberg, 28; Newscom: Photoshot/Xinhua/Zhaopeng, 33, Reuters/China Newsphoto, 10, Werner
Forman/akg-images, 37, Zuma Press/Ji Zhe, 40; Shutterstock: Aptyp_koK, cover (top right), fotohunter,
12–13, gary718, 38, hxdbzxy, 43, Jarno Gonzalez Zarraonandia, 15, Ke Wang, 4, Lukas Hlavac, 31,
Taily, cover (bottom right), Taweesak Thiprod, 18, Videowokart, cover (left); Wikimedia: BabelStone,
19, Public Domain, 25, vlasta2, 23; Wikipedia: Public Domain, 5, 6–7, 16

Design Elements: Shutterstock: LeshaBu, MADDRAT, renew studio

**Library of Congress Cataloging-in-Publication Data**
  Rosinsky, Natalie M. (Natalie Myra)
  Ancient China / by Natalie M. Rosinsky.
      p. cm.—(Exploring the ancient world)
  Includes bibliographical references and index.
  ISBN 978-0-7565-4568-0 (library binding)
  ISBN 978-0-7565-4578-9 (paperback)
  ISBN 978-0-7565-4623-6 (ebook PDF)
  1. China—Civilization—Juvenile literature. I. Title.
  DS706.R577 2013
  931—dc23                      2012001965

**Editor's Note:** Compass Point Books uses new abbreviations to
distinguish time periods. For ancient times, instead of BC, we
use BCE, which means before the common era. BC means before
Christ. Similarly, we use CE, which means in the common era,
instead of AD. The abbreviation AD stands for the Latin phrase
*anno Domini*, which means in the year of our Lord, referring to Jesus Christ.

Printed in the United States of America in Stevens Point, Wisconsin.

# Table of CONTENTS

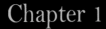

# Chapter 1

# COUNTRY of MARVELS and MYSTERIES

A stone and earthen wall thousands of miles long. A buried army of lifelike clay warriors, ready to defend the tomb of a great emperor. Amazing, world-changing inventions, including paper, movable type, and gunpowder. The history of ancient China is filled with such marvels and mysteries.

China is the third largest country in the world. It occupies 3.7 million square miles (9.6 million square kilometers) in

East Asia. China has mountain ranges and plains, rivers and deserts, grasslands and forests. Its long eastern border is the Pacific Ocean, where Chinese territory includes large and small islands. Fourteen nations border the rest of China.

China's size and shape have changed over time, as various emperors have ruled. The earliest Chinese people, dating back thousands of years, lived in the northern Yellow River Valley. Through warfare and sometimes marriage, each emperor and his dynasty would acquire or lose land. Historians have exciting stories to tell about the ancient dynasties.

Since the sixth century BCE, Chinese people often called their country the Middle Kingdom. They proudly believed their land to be the center of the civilized world. They even put China in the middle of their world maps. Sima Qian (ca. 145 to 86 BCE) had the job of "grand historian" for rulers. He inherited the job from his father, Sima Tan, who was pleased that his talented son would continue his unfinished work.

"Grand historian" Sima Qian

Thousands of life-size terra-cotta warriors, unearthed in 1974, guarded the ancient tomb of Emperor Qin Shi Huangdi.

# Chinese Dynasties

| | |
|---|---|
| Xia Dynasty (unconfirmed) | ca. 2100–1600 BCE |
| Shang Dynasty | ca. 1600–1050 BCE |
| Zhou Dynasty | ca. 1050–256 BCE |
| Qin Dynasty | 221–206 BCE |
| Han Dynasty | 206 BCE–220 CE |
| Six Dynasties | 220–589 |
| Sui Dynasty | 581–618 |

An early Ming Dynasty silk scroll portrays the legendary Yellow Emperor meeting with a religious leader.

| | |
|---|---|
| Tang Dynasty | 618–906 |
| Five Dynasties | 907–960 |
| Liao Dynasty | 907–1125 |
| Song Dynasty | 960–1279 |
| Yuan Dynasty | 1279–1368 |
| Ming Dynasty | 1368–1644 |
| Qing Dynasty | 1644–1911 |

Source: Heilbrunn Timeline of Art History, the Metropolitan Museum of Art, New York
www.metmuseum.org/toah/hd/chem/hd_chem.htm_

Present-day China

Shang Dynasty 1600-1050 BCE

In the last part of Sima Qian's famous book *Shiji* (*Historical Records*), he writes that he agreed, "bowing his head and weeping," to undertake the task. Sima Qian promised his aged father that he would "discuss everything ... concerning ancient times ... [and] not dare to leave any gaps in it."

Sima Qian's book included the early Shang dynasty, even though no palace records survived from that time. Some people thought Sima was only repeating folktales. They did not believe there had been a Shang Dynasty. But during an excavation in China that began in 1928, archeologists dug up proof that the Shang people had had a real kingdom. They discovered oracle bones the Shang had used to question the gods.

An oracle bone is a turtle shell or an animal bone that was used to practice fortune-telling. A bone or shell was heated until it cracked. The ancient Chinese believed that the pattern of cracks or other markings foretold the future.

Sima also wrote about an even

Han Dynasty 206 BCE-220 CE

Ming Dynasty 1368-1644 CE

earlier dynasty, the Xia. It may have begun around 2100 BCE. The Xia's first ruler was known as Yu the Great. An earlier figure, called the Yellow Emperor, seemed supernatural. Stories said he could change into a bear and stop flooding rivers using just his fingernails. The legendary Yellow Emperor also supposedly developed Chinese writing and first read oracle bones.

Many historians still call the Xia Dynasty imaginary. Yet modern archeologists have found city ruins from the time period when the Xia supposedly lived. Perhaps some of

Sima's history about the Xia—like his accounts of the Shang—will be proven by science.

China's vast, 5,000-year-old civilization is still revealing its secrets to archeologists and other scholars. As they learn more, historians argue about whether "ancient China" ended during the second, seventh, or 17th century. Many historians, though, continue to define ancient China as imperial China. That ended in 1911, when the last emperor ceased to rule. That is the definition of ancient China used in this book.

# Chapter 2

# Science and Technology

"Have pity on us soldiers, Treated as though we were not men!" These are lines from a song that was popular during the Zhou Dynasty (ca. 1050–256 BCE), but it also describes the treatment of ordinary soldiers during other dynasties. As rulers fought for territory and power in ancient China, they valued weapons more than foot soldiers. For many military leaders, there would always be more peasants or slaves to order into

battle. But chariots and bronze axes in the early dynasties were rare and precious.

Forging weapons and other objects out of bronze was one of the Shang Dynasty's (ca. 1600–1050 BCE) accomplishments. Its artisans developed a technology that used clay molds. Melted bronze was poured into the molds. When it cooled, the clay would be removed to reveal the finished bronze object, such as an ax or spearhead. Wealthy Shang nobles sometimes used these weapons to hunt large animals for sport. In wartime only the wealthy could use them. Ordinary Shang soldiers used inferior stone weapons. Early Shang farmers and others also usually used tools made of stone rather than valuable bronze.

A later invention did benefit people outside of the army. Iron forged for Zhou crossbows was also made into plows. The strong edges of the new plows, their plowshares, did not break the way wooden ones had. Farmers could more easily grow food to feed their families—and produce food for large armies. By the middle of the Han Dynasty (206 BCE–220 CE), iron plowshares and other iron tools were common. Even crossbows had a peaceful use. Archers used them to shoot sturdy cables across wide canyons. The cables were the first step in building hanging bridges.

An archeologist works in a pit in central China that holds chariots and horses from the Shang Dynasty.

The Qin Dynasty (221–206 BCE) lasted only 15 years, but it is widely believed that it gave China its modern name. (*Qin* is pronounced "Chin.") The strong personality of the dynasty's most famous leader is obvious in the grand name he chose for himself. King Zheng of Qin conquered and then united the surrounding kingdoms. Zheng declared he would be called Qin Shi Huangdi—"First Emperor" of the Qin dynasty. Only the legendary Yellow Emperor had ever held such a supreme title.

The Qin Emperor did both good and harm. A construction project he ordered to defend his empire from

northern invaders remains a marvel today. About 1,500 miles (2,414 kilometers) of China's Great Wall were built, or existing sections were linked, by workers under Qin Shi Huangdi's command. The east-to-west barrier, along with a few northern mountains and rivers, protected China from hordes of fierce nomads. But the accomplishment had what today would be considered a high price. Historians believe that more than a million people, forced to work in harsh conditions, died while building the towering, packed-earth wall. The cruel emperor did not care about their suffering.

The Great Wall is known to the Chinese as the Wan Li Chang Cheng, which translates to the Long Wall of Ten Thousand Li. Two li equal one kilometer.

The Qin Emperor built roads and had people appointed to government jobs based on their abilities rather than their family background. He demanded that officials keep written records and established a new money system. Its metal coins made trade—and collecting taxes—easier. Yet the emperor remained suspicious and fearful. While he had been King Zheng, there had been three attempts on his life. Two had occurred in the palace itself. How could he feel safe when even a blind musician tried to kill him with an iron harp? He outlawed the ownership of weapons by anyone except his soldiers. He collected all the private weapons in his empire and had their metal parts melted to make bells and 12 enormous statues for his palace.

But Qin Shi Huangdi remained uneasy. He ordered the burning of books that did not praise him. People who even talked about the banned books could "be executed and their bodies" left "in the marketplace." The emperor had scholars—perhaps more than 400—burned alive.

Qin Shi Huangdi sought to guarantee an afterlife by building a magnificent tomb. Thousands of life-size terra-cotta warriors, their war horses, bronze weapons, and chariots, were buried with him and guarded the tomb. The guards were so finely detailed that their clay "clothing" even showed plated armor, the latest imperial fashion. Thousands of workers may have died—some during construction and others killed later to ensure the tomb's location was never revealed. Its marvels remained buried until 1974, when well-diggers accidentally uncovered parts of the site.

The Han Dynasty, which followed the Qin, brought more inventions useful in war and peace. Wheelbarrows were first used to transport army supplies and wounded soldiers, but they later helped farmers. Leather collars and harnesses were created for chariot horses, but leather harnesses for oxen let them more easily pull farm carts. These

The terra-cotta warriors were buried for more than 2,000 years. Each figure is unique.

aids came into use around 100 BCE, when Chinese farmers began using chain pumps to irrigate land. The pumps' wooden paddles moved water from one level of land to another. Rice grown on the irrigated land fed civilians as well as soldiers.

New technology at this time also helped the Chinese preserve food. Without refrigeration, people used salt to keep meat from spoiling. Clever salt miners used iron drill heads to dig deep into the earth to reach salt water. The water was pumped up and boiled in large, flat iron pans until it evaporated and only precious salt crystals remained. Salt was so valuable that the Han government for a while took control of the salt- and iron-making businesses. After miners accidentally dug into pockets of natural gas, they put the gas to good use. Some salt miners burned gas to heat their iron pans. Other ancient Chinese used bamboo pipes to light their villages with natural gas. Western countries did not have gaslights until 17 centuries later.

Some scientific inventions received imperial support for nonscientific reasons. Later Han emperors wanted to know whether the gods still favored them. Such a "mandate of heaven" was important to keep their subjects loyal and obedient. The rulers asked questions about why "the earth shook" and "rivers dried up" under their rule. What could they learn and predict about natural events? Such knowledge

Tomb sculpture of a Han Dynasty farmer

might be used to show that a ruler had the approval of heaven.

Scientist and court official Zhang Heng (78–139 CE) invented the first machine that could give early warning of earthquakes. The bronze seismometer showed even small vibrations using a series of delicately balanced balls. When the ground shook the balls dropped from the mouths of molded dragons into the gaping mouths of bronze frogs. Zhang Heng also studied mathematics and the movement of stars.

Scientists and inventors continued their efforts. When facing questions about life and death, though, some people looked to religion and philosophy for answers.

Model of Zhang Heng's seismometer

# Chapter 3

# Religion and Philosophy

"Heaven, earth, and man are the source of all creatures. Heaven gives birth to them, earth nourishes them, and human beings complete them."

Philosopher Dong Zhongshu (179–104 BCE) could have been describing Chinese religion with this remark. The ancient Chinese believed in a creator god called Di, but they also worshipped earth spirits. Many people believed that the spirits of their ancestors watched over them. There were special rituals to ask for the help of ancestors and spirits. Sometimes the rituals involved asking questions about the future using oracle bones or directions in a book called the *Yijing (Book of Changes)*. The Chinese also believed that an honorable emperor had special approval, called a mandate, from Tian, which means heaven. That is why one of an emperor's titles was "son of heaven."

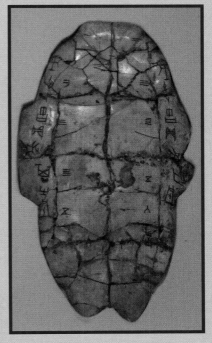

An oracle bone from the Shang Dynasty is made from a turtle shell.

There was a pantheon of minor gods that some Chinese worshipped. During later dynasties the pantheon also included gods from foreign religions. That is when statues and other images of gods became part of Chinese art. Yet the three major beliefs that came to dominate Chinese culture are not directly part of this traditional, complex religion.

One belief is Confucianism. "Do not do unto others what you would not have them do unto you. Then neither in your country nor in your family will there be complaints against you." This wise saying was one of many spoken by philosopher and teacher Kong Fuzi (Master Kong), who lived from 551 to 479 BCE. The sayings are collected in a book called the *Analects*. It and three other books written by followers of

Guanyin, the Buddhist goddess of compassion, was introduced in China during the late Han Dynasty.

Confucius—as Kong Fuzi became known in the West—had an enormous impact on imperial China. The books spread Confucius' belief in human goodness, the importance of duty and respect, and the value of study and education. Confucius practiced these values as a government official and famous teacher. In his own words, "By fifteen I was intent on learning; by thirty I was standing straight; by forty I was no longer confused; by fifty I knew heaven's commands ..." Confucius' students became important teachers and government officials.

The Qin Emperor Shi Huangdi did not believe in or practice Confucian values. This powerful ruler controlled his subjects through fear, not kindness. He established a strong, strict system of laws and punishment. It outlawed Confucianism. The books Qin Shi Huangdi burned included the *Analects*, and Confucian scholars risked their lives. Only when Liu Bang, the first emperor of the Han Dynasty, gained power was it again safe to be Confucian.

Liu Bang's great-grandson, Emperor Wu Di, went further. In 136 BCE he made Confucianism the official belief of his empire. Around 124 BCE he established an imperial university to train government officials in Confucianism. The school was open to all. Even commoners— if they passed examinations on Confucian books—could obtain high positions in China's expanding government. This national civil service examination system was used in China until 1905.

After the Han Dynasty, during what became known as the period of disunity, few young men bothered to study for the exams. During the Tang Dynasty (618–906 CE), though, superior Confucian scholars again became important government advisers and officials. The next

Confucius lectured to his students, who in turn, became teachers.

dynasties also respected Confucian knowledge and values.

Daoism, which means "the Path" or "the Way," was the second significant belief in ancient China. Daoism, also known as Taoism, urged people to imitate the supposedly peaceful and quiet ways of nature. Unlike Confucianism, Daoism did not urge competition and activity. It did not seek to influence society. A well-known

Daoist saying is that "water benefits all creatures but does not compete. It occupies the places people disdain and thus comes near to the Way." Another Daoist saying is "Engage in no action and order will prevail."

These statements come from an early and important Daoist book titled the *Daodejing (The Classic of the Way and Its Virtue)*. It may have been written by a contemporary of Confucius, the scholar Laozi.

The harmony in nature valued by Daoism is often described as a balance between opposing forces. Traditional Chinese medicine tries to balance these forces—called yin and yang—to produce health and long life. The forces are often shown as dark and light halves of a circle.

According to the historian Sima Qian, the philosopher Laozi lived in the sixth century BCE. Another ancient book says Confucius met and talked with this Daoist teacher. Yet some scholars think the real Laozi lived 200 years later. Some people question whether Laozi existed at all.

The name Laozi means

A modern postage stamp featured the philosopher Laozi.

# New Looks for Books

The books Confucius read looked nothing like the one you are reading. From around 500 BCE until about 105 CE, Chinese books usually were made of long, thin bamboo strips. Cords held the strips together. It was said that Confucius studied the *Book of Changes* so much that the leather cords "binding the . . . strips wore out three times." Scholars handwrote Chinese characters using slim brushes and black ink. During Confucius' lifetime, a few books were written on a newly invented material, silk.

But it was the invention of paper in 105 CE that gave books a whole new look. Paper books weighed much less than bamboo books and could be transported more easily. A Han official named Cai Lun supposedly invented paper. Chinese inventors later gave books two other new looks. The first printed book was

Bamboo book

wood block-printed by hand around 868. The Chinese invented movable type around 1040—about 400 years before Johannes Gutenberg perfected his movable type printing press in Germany.

"Old Master." The name and extraordinary stories told about Laozi's life may have been made up to pass along the shared beliefs of several scholars. For instance, it is said that Laozi lived to a remarkable old age. Some legends have him writing the *Daodejing* in just one night. After that, he is supposed to have vanished into India to continue teaching there, where Buddha may have been his student.

Buddhism is the third belief system that became important in China. This religion spread to China from India in the first century CE. That is where Buddhism's founder, a prince named Siddhartha Gautama, lived. According to tradition, he was born in northern India, in what is now Nepal, in 563 BCE. Because of the holy life he chose and his peaceful teachings, he became known as the Buddha—meaning "Enlightened One" or "Awakened One."

Buddhists, like Daoists, did not value possessions or worldly success. They believed suffering was part of life, and they followed an eightfold path of right behavior, thought, and meditation. Buddhists believed that through their actions they would be continually reborn after death until they finally achieved a kind of salvation known as nirvana.

Buddhism spread widely in China from the late Han Dynasty through the Song Dynasty. It brought new gods into the pantheon of traditional Chinese religion. One important god was Guanyin, the goddess of compassion. She appears in a famous Tang Dynasty novel called *Journey to the West*. Its popular heroes include a mischief-making minor god, the Monkey King. Buddhism also inspired artists and crafts workers.

A mural depicts Emperor Xuan Wu Di worshipping statues of the Buddha. The mural is one of many in the ancient Mogao cave temples near Dunhuang.

# Chapter 4

# Crafting Daily Life

"Men plow and women weave." This folk saying from the Zhou period or earlier was true in several ways in ancient China. Weaving cloth was women's work. In fact, girls and women were involved in

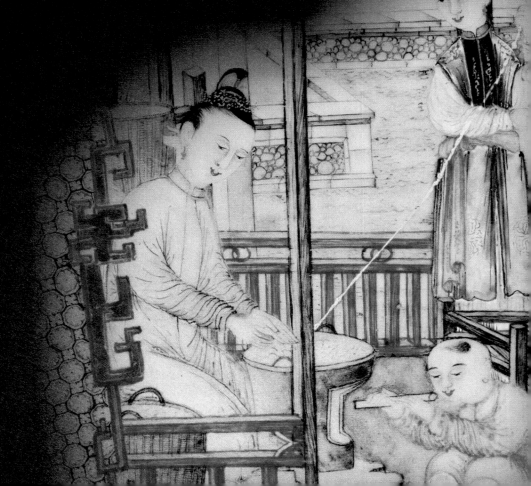

all stages of silk production. There was a lot to do before the delicate cloth could be woven.

They tended the silkworms, separated silk fibers from their cocoons, and spun them into thread. Information about silk production was a state secret. For several thousand years, emperors forbade taking the information or silkworms out of China. This protected China's monopoly on silk, which was a valuable trade item.

Despite their important role in silk making, though, women usually could not participate in daily activities open to men. This is the other truth in that old folk saying. Except in the poorest families, women did not plow. Young women could not attend school, take examinations, and become government officials. When printing made more books available, the change did not benefit most curious or ambitious girls. Instead Confucianism kept women apart from the four traditional social classes. The highest class was scholars, followed by farmers, artisans, and merchants.

Women were supposed to be dutiful and helpful daughters, wives, and mothers. Girls and women were supposed to obey first their fathers and then their husbands. A later change in fashion further limited Chinese women's lives. During and after the Song Dynasty (960–1279), many girls lost the ability to walk easily. Their feet were bound, broken, and shaped to look like small lotus petals, which people thought looked pretty.

Detail from a Ming Dynasty vase depicting women spinning silk

Fine silk garments typically were not found in ordinary homes. On farms and in villages, most people wore cotton or linen garments. Their dishes, furniture, and household shrines were not elaborate or made of the most expensive materials. Apart from the homes of village officials, fine arts and crafts usually shone brightest in cities. Two of ancient China's largest cities were also imperial capitals.

Xi'an, which was called Chang'an before the Ming Dynasty (1368–1644), is one of the oldest capital cities of China. Around 202 BCE, the first Han emperor ordered its expansion. He established the imperial university there. At its height, Xi'an was as large and had as many inhabitants as ancient Rome—more than a million people.

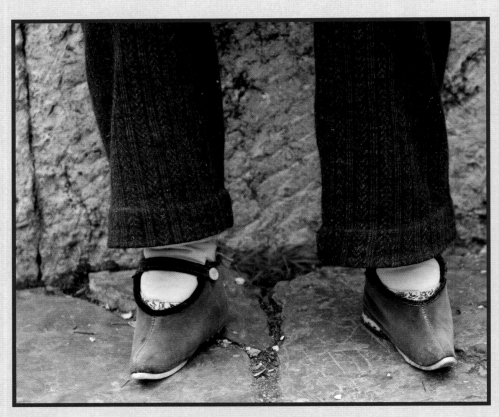

A 90-year-old woman is one of the last survivors of the banned practice of foot binding.

# Two Remarkable Women

Some women in ancient China overcame tradition with good luck, ability, and determination. Wu Zetian (625–705) was the only female emperor of ancient China. She had been the ambitious concubine of a Tang Dynasty emperor. Through intelligence, cunning, and—possibly—murder, she ruled China in her own name for 15 years, from 690 to 705. She supported artists, musicians, and poets, and she herself wrote poetry.

Wu Zetian

Ban Zhao (ca. 45–116) was fortunate to be the daughter of a Confucian scholar and sister of a court historian. She received a fine education. When her brother died, Ban Zhao completed his *Annals* for the Han emperor. Among other works, Ban Zhao also wrote an instruction book for young women titled *Lessons for Women*. She hoped its practical advice would help young wives avoid the "trembling heart" she had had as a bride, when "at the age of fourteen [she] took up the dustpan and the broom" in her new husband's family home. Ban Zhao was unusual for her time—a famous and successful female Confucian scholar.

# Colorful Traditions

In Chinese art and society, the color bright yellow was reserved for emperors and their families. White was associated with death and mourning. Red was the color of good fortune. By tradition, various creatures had special meanings too. Dragons represented strength and goodness. Another mythological creature called the phoenix stood for long life and good luck, as did real, long-legged cranes. Butterflies represented young love. Certain flowers carried special meanings as well.

A colorful dragon adorns a Ming Dynasty vase.

Ban Zhao and Empress Wu both lived there. Palace builders then and later followed the ancient rules of feng shui. This system helps people design buildings and rooms that supposedly bring inhabitants good luck and spiritual harmony.

Beijing was first declared China's capital in the 13th century, and it remains the capital today. At times it has been the largest city in the world. Between 1405 and 1421, the Ming emperor built an elaborate imperial palace there. Called the Forbidden City, the palace contained nearly 1,000 decorated wooden buildings. Their indoor decorations included wooden panels and silk screens painted with beautiful landscapes. Wall hangings displayed beautiful, complicated handwriting called calligraphy.

Twenty-four emperors lived in the Forbidden City between 1420 and 1912.

Fine arts and crafts often showcased a dynasty's new technology and beliefs. That is why—in addition to valued bronze and precious jade—wealthy Tang era homes and even tombs contained beautiful blue vases. They were made of cobalt blue porcelain, which was a Tang Dynasty creation.

Similarly, Yuan and Ming leaders were proud of their special blue and white patterned porcelain. As Buddhism became important to some ancient Chinese, Buddhist art also appeared in grand homes as well as temples.

Chinese artists inspired by Buddhism used materials and techniques typical of their era. At first, statues of the Buddha were crafted from purest stone or bronze. Many were made during the Sui Dynasty (581–618), when many Buddhist temples were built. That is also when some people retreated to Buddhist meditation caves. By the Song

Detail from a Ming Dynasty vase depicting potters making porcelain bowls

Dynasty, statues of the Buddha and other Buddhist figures, such as Guanyin, were also being made of finely carved, painted wood. Such carvings were then a new, highly prized accomplishment. Often the Buddha was shown seated in a meditating position. He had achieved enlightenment while meditating. As trade expanded inside and outside ancient China, more people came to value Chinese arts, crafts, and inventions.

Reliefs carved more than 1,000 years ago in the Gongyi Grotto Temple depict the emperor and queen worshipping the Buddha. The site contains nearly 8,000 Buddha statues.

# Chapter 5

# Trade and Change Across the Centuries

"The custom in the North is to avoid direct criticisms. …You boys should be careful not to give your opinions too freely." A southern Chinese father gave this advice to his sons around 575. Differences in Chinese customs, though, soon grew less important. Trade and the desire for conquest changed the face of ancient China.

Between 605 and 609, the Sui emperor had the Grand Canal dug. The waterway, which stretched nearly 1,200 miles (1,930 km) from north to south, made it easier to trade goods and move army supplies. New

roads also united areas that once had been at war. One changed custom involved tea. Once used as a southern medicine, tea became a popular social drink throughout China.

During the Tang Dynasty, trade and growth continued. Empress Wu was just one of the rulers who expanded the empire. The Grand Canal remained important. Ming leaders repaired and lengthened it in the 16th century.

Trade across international borders along an east-to-west series of routes called the Silk Road also flourished. Between about 600 and 1400, thousands of traders traveled from Xi'an in western China to the city of Samarkand in what today is Uzbekistan and on to what would become the capital of the Muslim world, Baghdad. Chinese silk—prized by Westerners since the second century BCE—was one of the most valuable trade items on the more than 4,000-mile (6,437-km) route. Its production still remained a mystery outside China.

Chinese tea, porcelains, and gunpowder (invented around 850) were also highly prized trading goods. In return, merchants brought back to China fine glass from Baghdad, ivory and spices from India, and gold and silver crafts from Arab lands. Goods might begin a journey from Xi'an in ox carts, but camels hauled traders and goods through the deserts of western China to dusty Samarkand and Baghdad. Important ideas sometimes traveled this way too. Knowledge about papermaking and the stars spread westward from China.

Boats on the Grand Canal carried grain from the south to cities and armies in the north.

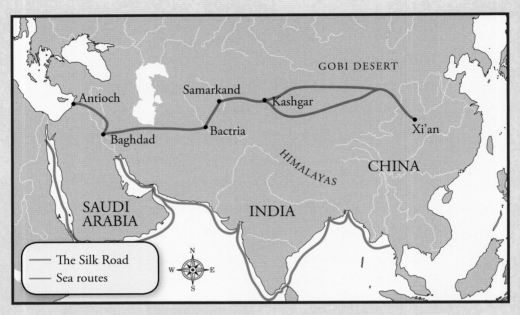

GOBI DESERT

Antioch

Samarkand

Kashgar

Baghdad

Bactria

Xi'an

HIMALAYAS

CHINA

SAUDI
ARABIA

INDIA

—— The Silk Road
—— Sea routes

N
W E
S

The Silk Road was not one highway but a series of routes across China
and the Middle East. Its routes changed through the centuries.

Traders included Turks and Arabs. Italian Marco Polo was one of the first Europeans to venture deep into China. After his return home in 1295, Polo's stories and the goods he brought back increased European interest in trading with China. Christopher Columbus and other explorers hoped to find a quick, easy sea route to China by sailing west. This led to Europe's "discovering" the new world of the Americas.

Chinese inventions helped make these long voyages possible. One was the magnetic compass, which was first used for navigation about 1100. Another Chinese invention was a rudder to steer boats and ships. It first appeared in China in the first century CE.

China continued to attract interest from powerful people and nations. In the 13th century, the Mongol leader Genghis Khan (Cheng Ji Si Han) conquered large parts of China. His grandson Kubla Khan (Hubilie Han) later established the Yuan Dynasty (1279–1368). Marco Polo visited China during Kubla Khan's reign.

Some emperors during the following Ming Dynasty, though, tried to limit foreign influence. They stopped Chinese exploration westward too. Their generally successful efforts included strengthening and lengthening the Great Wall. The Ming Dynasty finally fell in 1644, however, to powerful men from the northern region of Manchuria.

The Manchu Qing Dynasty lasted more than 250 years, until 1911. During the 1800s Qing leaders faced increased European attempts to profit from China. One of these schemes led to the Opium Wars of the 1840s and 1850s. Britain wanted China to open its ports to foreign trade. China wanted to keep out foreign trade and ban the import of opium. The drug was grown in India,

which Britain controlled. China lost these conflicts. At that point, the marvels of ancient China could not withstand the British Empire's power and ambition. Later, however, ancient China would have a huge impact on the modern world.

Genghis Khan overpowering a fortress; from a 1590 Persian history book

# Chapter 6

# Ancient China in Today's World

The 20th century saw huge changes, including a revolution in 1911 that ended the Chinese empire. China experienced more war and turbulence, including a brutal Communist dictatorship. Today it is a growing, powerful country. China's national wealth is important worldwide. The success of Chinese who have immigrated to other countries also often draws attention. Even before these

newsworthy events, though, ancient China helped shape today's world.

Ancient China's influence extends far beyond the many museums that display its arts and crafts. It has affected today's world in ways both big and small. Without the Chinese invention of gunpowder, the history of warfare and rise of nations might have been different. Paper and movable type are other inventions that helped shape today's world. Ancient China's many achievements in science and technology are enough to fill a whole encyclopedia—and they do! The 24-volume *Science and Civilization in Ancient China* begun by historian Joseph Needham in 1954 is still adding volumes.

Confucianism continues to be important to the Chinese. Buddhism today is a major worldwide religion, and Daoism is a philosophy that is also studied worldwide. Chinese traditional medicine—drawing upon the Daoist principles of yin and yang—is not only practiced in modern China. Its use of herbs and acupuncture is respected by many Western doctors too. Some worldwide exercise practices such as tai chi also draw upon these principles. The yin-yang symbol decorates jewelry, clothing, advertising signs, and the South Korean flag. The related ideas of feng shui continue to influence architecture and home design around the globe. Its principles are on display in Beijing's Forbidden City, now a famous museum.

Fireworks explode over Tiananmen Square in Beijing.

A pharmacist prepares traditional Chinese medicine in eastern China.

An ancient book of military strategy, written by a general who lived in the sixth century BCE, has remained important. The author of *Art of War* is usually considered to be Sun Wu, better known as Sun Tzu. The book inspired Vietnamese leaders in their fight for independence in the middle of the last century. The U.S. military uses *Art of War* to train its forces. In recent years several authors have written books about achieving business or personal success based on Sun Tzu's strategic use of Daoism.

# Chinese Writing

On some old maps, you may see China's capital city written as Peking. New maps show a city named Beijing as the capital. Newer books in English also spell Chinese names differently than older books. This seeming mystery is easy to explain.

Chinese writing has never used the Western alphabet. It uses characters that originally were pictures of the things or activities they described. Instead of 26 letters, there are thousands of such characters.

Western writers had to find a common way to spell Chinese names and words. The Wade-Giles system was widely used until the 1960s. In it, the name of China's capital city is Peking. In 1979 the Chinese government officially adopted a new system called Pinyin. It is based on the Mandarin dialect of the Chinese language. Pinyin has many differences—for instance, in Pinyin China's capital is spelled Beijing. That is closer to the way speakers of Mandarin Chinese pronounce the city's name.

Chinese foods are popular around the globe. Many holidays and special events today are celebrated with fireworks, another invention of the ancient Chinese. Their dazzling displays followed the invention of gunpowder. Even such everyday items as toilet paper and matches might be traceable to ancient China. It is said that Chinese women invented matches during a sixth century war, when tinder to start fires was scarce.

# Admiral and Diplomat

An ancient Chinese admiral—using the Chinese inventions of magnetic compasses and seaworthy rudders—traveled farther, and with many more and much larger ships, than Christopher Columbus ever did. Between 1405 and 1433, Admiral Zheng He commanded 317 ships on seven long sea voyages to Southeast Asia and Africa. Some ships were as big as a football field. Zheng He visited 37 countries, where he gained their leaders' loyalty for the Ming emperor and spread Chinese culture. Zheng He's success is all the more remarkable because of his humble beginnings. As a Muslim child born on the outskirts of China, he had been brutally enslaved at the age of 10. He rose to a position of power through his many talents.

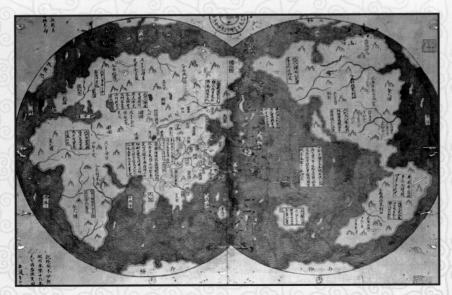

A world map some historians believe was compiled by Zheng He in 1418

If you enjoy fun and games, you may want to thank the ancient Chinese. They are believed to have invented playing cards and kites. There are records of a ninth century Tang Dynasty princess playing a card game.

The Chinese also popularized high-flying kites. Flown first as cries for help during wartime, kites during the Tang and Ming dynasties became objects of skill and beauty. Think about that the next time a kite soars high above your head!

A kite soars above the Chinese city of Shanghai.

# Timeline

| | |
|---|---|
| **1600–1050 BCE** | Oracle bones are used and bronze weapons and objects are forged during the Shang Dynasty |
| **500s BCE** | Time during which Laozi is said to have lived |
| **551 BCE** | Confucius is born |
| **221–206 BCE** | Emperor Quin Shi Huangdi unites China; sections of the Great Wall are built and existing sections linked |
| **136 BCE** | Confucianism becomes the official belief system |
| **100s BCE** | Leather harnesses, wheelbarrows, chain pumps, iron tools, and salt and gas mining become common; the seismometer and paper are invented |
| **104–91 BCE** | Sima Qian writes *Shiji (Historical Records)* |
| **200s CE** | Buddhism spreads throughout China |
| **600–1400** | The Silk Road is at its height |
| **605–609** | The Grand Canal is built |
| **850** | Gunpowder is invented |
| **960** | Foot binding becomes a fashion; porcelain factories are built |
| **1040** | Movable type is invented |
| **1100** | The magnetic compass is first used for navigation |
| **1215** | Mongol invader Genghis Khan conquers Beijing |
| **1400–1664** | The Grand Canal and Great Wall are expanded |
| **1405–1433** | Admiral Zheng He visits 37 countries during his sea voyages |
| **1840-1850s** | China loses the Opium Wars with Great Britain |
| **1911** | The last emperor is deposed |

# Glossary

**acupuncture**—treatment in traditional Chinese medicine that uses needles at special points on the human body to control pain and cure disease

**artisan**—someone who is skilled in a craft, especially one whose occupation requires hand skill

**cobalt**—silver-white metal element used for blue glass and ceramic pigments; the blue color is also produced by artisans using a special heating process

**compassion**—awareness of and sympathy for human suffering, along with a desire to help those who are suffering

**concubine**—in imperial China, a woman who lived with a man as his secondary wife; a concubine had few legal rights and a lower social position than a wife

**dialect**—regional form of a language that may differ from other dialects in vocabulary and pronunciation

**dynasty**—generations of rulers from the same family

**imperial**—part of an empire or belonging to an emperor or empress

**meditation**—process of focusing one's attention to increase personal awareness, religious or spiritual understanding, or physical health

**monopoly**—having exclusive control over something or some service

**nomads**—people without fixed homes who travel within a territory according to the seasons

**pantheon**—officially recognized gods of a people

**shrines**—places of religious worship or devotion

**strategy**—plan or series of plans to reach a major goal, sometimes a military one

**terra-cotta**—hard, red-brown clay, often used for statues or pots

# Select Bibliography

The Art of Asia—Resources. Minneapolis Institute of Arts. 27 April 2012. www.artsmia.org/art-of-asia/history/

Cotterell, Arthur. *China: A Cultural History.* New York: New American Library, 1988.

Cotterell, Arthur. *The Imperial Capitals of China: A Dynastic History of the Celestial Empire.* Woodstock, N.Y.: Overlook Press, 2008.

Cotterell, Arthur, and David Morgan. *China's Civilization: A Survey of Its History, Arts, and Technology.* New York: Praeger, 1975.

Dawson, Raymond, trans. and ed. *Historical Records/Sima Qian.* Oxford: Oxford University Press, 1994.

De Bary, William Theodore, and Irene Bloom. *Sources of Chinese Tradition,* 2nd ed., vol. 1. New York: Columbia University Press, 1999.

Ebrey, Patricia Buckley. *The Cambridge Illustrated History of China,* 2nd ed. Cambridge: Cambridge University Press, 2010.

Ebrey, Patricia Buckley, ed. *Chinese Civilization: A Sourcebook,* 2nd ed. New York: Free Press, 1993.

Ebrey, Patricia Buckley. *Women and the Family in Chinese History.* London: Routledge, 2003.

Kleeman, Terry, and Tracy Barrett. *The Ancient Chinese World.* Oxford: Oxford University Press, 2005.

Liu, Xinru. *The Silk Road in World History.* Oxford: Oxford University Press, 2010.

The Silk Road—Ancient Pathway to the Modern World. American Museum of Natural History. 27 April 2012. www.amnh.org/exhibitions/silkroad/journey.php

The Silk Road Foundation. 27 April 2012. www.silkroadfoundation.org/toc/index.html

Swimming Dragons. BBC Radio. 3 June 2011. 27 April 2012. www.bbc.co.uk/radio4/history/swimming_dragons.shtml

Szuma, Chien. *Records of the Historian.* Yang Hsienn-ji and Gladys Yang, trans. Hong Kong: The Commercial Press, 1974.

Winchester, Simon. *The Man Who Loved China: The Fantastic Story of the Eccentric Scientist Who Unlocked the Mysteries of the Middle Kingdom.* New York: Harper, 2008.

Wing, R.L. *The Art of Strategy: A New Translation of Sun Tzu's Classic* The Art of War. New York: Doubleday, 1988.

Wu, K.C. *The Chinese Heritage.* New York: Crown, 1982.

# Source Notes

Page 8, line 4: Raymond Dawson, trans. and ed. *Historical Records/Sima Qian.* Oxford: Oxford University Press, 1994, p. xx.

Page 10, line 1: Patricia Buckley Ebrey, ed. *Chinese Civilization: A Sourcebook,* 2nd ed. New York: Free Press, 1993, p. 13.

Page 14, line 26: William Theodore de Bary and Irene Bloom. *Sources of Chinese Tradition,* 2nd ed., vol. 1. New York: Columbia University Press, 1999, p. 210.

Page 16, line 24: Arthur Cotterell. *China: A Cultural History.* New York: New American Library, 1988, p. 29.

Page 18, line 1: *Chinese Civilization: A Sourcebook,* p. 57.

Page 19, line 19: Patricia Buckley Ebrey. *The Cambridge Illustrated History of China,* 2nd ed. Cambridge: Cambridge University Press, 2010, p. 47.

Page 20, line 11: Ibid., p. 46.

Page 22, line 1: *The Cambridge Illustrated History of China,* p. 48.

Page 22, line 5: Ibid.

Page 23, line 5: Chien Szuma. *Records of the Historian.* Yang Hsienn-ji and Gladys Yang, trans. Hong Kong: The Commercial Press, 1974, p. 22.

Page 26, line 1: *The Cambridge Illustrated History of China,* p. 54.

Page 29, line 20: Nancy Lee Swann. *Pan Chao: Foremost Woman Scholar of China, First Century A.D.* New York: The Century Co., 1932, pp. 82–90. Excerpted on Brooklyn College Core 9: Chinese Culture Page. http://academic.brooklyn.cuny.edu/core9/phalsall/texts/banzhao.html

Page 34, line 1: *Chinese Civilization: A Sourcebook,* p. 111.

# Further Reading

Ball, Jacqueline, and Richard Levey. *Ancient China: Archaeology Unlocks the Secrets of China's Past.*
    Washington, D.C.: National Geographic, 2007.

Cotterell, Arthur. *Ancient China.*
    New York: DK Publishing, 2005.

DuTemple, Lesley A. *The Great Wall of China.*
    Minneapolis: Lerner Publications, 2003.

Fisher, Leonard Everett. *The Gods and Goddesses of Ancient China.*
    New York: Holiday House, 2003.

Greenblatt, Miriam. *Han Wu Di and Ancient China.*
    Tarrytown, N.Y.: Marshall Cavendish Benchmark, 2006.

Hall, Eleanor. J. *Ancient Chinese Dynasties.*
    San Diego, Calif.: Lucent Books, 2000.

Kleeman, Terry, and Tracy Barrett. *The Ancient Chinese World.*
    Oxford, U.K. and New York:.Oxford University Press, 2005.

Mah, Adeline Yen. *China: Land of Dragons and Emperors.*
    New York: Delacorte Press, 2008.

Marx, Trish. *Elephants and Golden Thrones: Inside China's Forbidden City.*
    New York: Abrams Books for Young Readers, 2008.

# On the Web

Use FactHound to find Internet sites related to this book. All of the sites on FactHound have been researched by our staff.

Here's all you do:

Visit www.facthound.com

Type in this code: 9780756545680

# Titles in this Series:

*The Byzantine Empire*
*Ancient China*
*Ancient Egypt*
*Ancient Greece*
*The Ancient Maya*
*Mesopotamia*

# Index

## About the Author

Natalie M. Rosinsky is an award-winning author of many books, articles, and activities for young readers, including a biography of Chinese-American author Amy Tan. A resident of Bloomington, Minnesota, Natalie enjoys visiting the splendid collections of Asian art at the Minneapolis Institute of Arts. Natalie learned to appreciate handcrafted Chinese furniture by seeing the delight it brought her parents, Fay and Sam Rosinsky.